When you pray, move your feet. —African proverb

For my B'more homies. Stay strong.
—C.B.W.

To Jacqui, my Mom/Cuz, my Angel
—L.F.

"I SAY TO OUR CHILDREN, DON'T LET ANYBODY TAKE AWAY YOUR HOPE.
I DON'T CARE WHO THEY ARE. AND LET NO ONE DEFINE YOU. NO ONE."
—ELIJAH CUMMINGS

Text copyright © 2021 by Carole Boston Weatherford
Jacket art and interior illustrations copyright © 2021 by Laura Freeman
Timeline photo: Elijah Eugene Cummings, Photographic print, color (chromogenic), ca 1995, Collection of the U.S. House of Representatives

Visit us on the Web! rhcbooks.com

Educators and librarians, for a variety of teaching tools, visit us at RHTeachersLibrarians.com

Library of Congress Cataloging-in-Publication Data
Names: Weatherford, Carole Boston, author. | Freeman, Laura, illustrator.
Title: The faith of Elijah Cummings : the north star of equal justice / by Carole Boston Weatherford ; illustrated by Laura Freeman.
Description: First edition. | New York : Random House Studio, [2021] | Includes bibliographical references. | Audience: Ages: 6–9 | Audience: Grades: 1–4 |
Summary: "A picture book biography of Elijah Cummings, outlining major events in his childhood, career, and fight for justice" —Provided by publisher
Identifiers: LCCN 2020032889 (print) | LCCN 2020032890 (ebook) | ISBN 978-0-593-30650-5 (hardcover) |
ISBN 978-0-593-30651-2 (library binding) | ISBN 978-0-593-30652-9 (ebook)
Subjects: LCSH: Cummings, Elijah—Juvenile literature. | United States. Congress. House—Biography—Juvenile literature. | African American legislators—
Maryland—Biography—Juvenile literature. | African American civil rights workers—Biography—Juvenile literature.
Classification: LCC E185.97.C966 W43 2021 (print) | LCC E185.97.C966 (ebook) | DDC 328.73/092 [B]—dc23

The text of this book is set in 13-point Sagona Book.
The illustrations in this book were created using Adobe Photoshop.
Book design by Nicole de las Heras

MANUFACTURED IN CHINA

10 9 8 7 6 5 4 3 2 1

First Edition

The author would like to thank Dr. Maya Rockeymoore Cummings
for her help with the information in this book.

THE FAITH OF ELIJAH CUMMINGS

The North Star of Equal Justice

written by
Carole Boston Weatherford

illustrated by
Laura Freeman

RANDOM HOUSE STUDIO ■ NEW YORK

REMARKS BY NANCY PELOSI,
SPEAKER OF THE U.S. HOUSE OF REPRESENTATIVES

October 25, 2019

How brilliant was it of Elijah's parents to name him Elijah? . . . There is a tradition to leave a seat at the table for [the prophet] Elijah, who might show up. But our Elijah always made a seat at the table for others.

He made a seat at the table for children who needed an education. For . . . new Members of Congress, so that he could mentor them. For all that wanted to be part of the American Dream. Elijah himself personally lived the American Dream, and he wanted everyone else to have that opportunity, hence many seats at the table. . . .

Elijah was a proud man: proud of his heritage, proud of Baltimore, and proud of America. He always appealed to our better angels and to the promise of America, calling us to live up to our principles and for a higher purpose.

He held himself to a high standard, and that is why I have called him "the North Star of Congress," our guiding light. . . .

In his Chairmanship on the Committee on Oversight and Reform, he lived up to his responsibilities to hold the Federal government accountable to the laws of the land.

One word I would use to describe Elijah over and over again is the word future. He was there to make the future for our children. . . . He wanted for those children to have a future worthy of their aspirations, and he wanted them to have a future built on our values. . . .

By example, he gave people hope. By his courage, he fought for what was right. By his brilliance, knowledge, and legal prowess, he made a difference in so many ways, fighting for gun violence prevention, expanding opportunity for everyone. . . .

God truly blessed America with the life and legacy of Elijah E. Cummings, mentor, master of the House, North Star, Mr. Chairman. . . .

"I HAD RIGHTS AND . . .
I HAD TO FIGHT FOR THEM."

IN THE SUMMER OF 1962, eleven-year-old Elijah Cummings and other African American children protested to integrate a city pool in Baltimore. As they marched to the pool, a white mob throwing rocks and bottles yelled, "Go back where you came from!"

The march—organized by Juanita Jackson Mitchell, a local civil rights lawyer—led Elijah to consider becoming a lawyer.

"THEY HAD FAITH THAT GOD
WAS LEADING THEM TO
A PLACE WHERE THEIR CHILDREN
WOULD HAVE A BETTER
CHANCE IN LIFE."

Racism was the very reason Elijah's sharecropper parents had moved north in the first place. In South Carolina, Ruth Cummings and her husband, Robert, each earned about fifteen cents an hour working on land where their ancestors had been enslaved.

Ruth had seen Blacks beaten for seeking voting rights. To escape this fate, the couple settled in Maryland in the 1940s.

"MY MOM AND DAD . . .
WERE TWO OF THE
MOST BRILLIANT PEOPLE."

In South Baltimore, Robert, Ruth, and their seven children lived in a rented four-room row house. They all shared one bathroom.

In cramped quarters, Elijah's parents—who only finished fourth grade—raised their children to value education. Robert had a saying: "If you miss a day of school, that means you died the night before."

Despite having perfect attendance, Elijah struggled in school. His teachers thought he talked too much and asked too many questions. They said he would never be able to read or write well.

Studying at home was tough. "Our house was so small," said Elijah, "that we children had to go to the library to do our homework."

Elijah found not only study space there, but also hope. The public library was one of the few places he went where both Black and white people could go. After the librarians got off work, they stayed on to tutor him. With their help, he proved his teachers wrong and returned to regular classes.

"THE LIBRARIANS AND BOOKS . . . DID SOMETHING MORE THAN TEACH ME HISTORY AND ENGLISH AND MATH. THEY HELPED ME DEFINE MYSELF AS A HUMAN BEING. THEY BECAME THE ROLE MODELS FOR MY LIFE."

At home, Elijah learned lessons about hard work and sacrifice.
His father was a laborer for a chemical company. His mother
worked at a pickle plant and later as a domestic, cleaning
other people's homes.

Ruth and Robert scrimped and saved so they could buy a house with more space and a grassy yard. This meant they could not afford Christmas presents for the children. Instead, Elijah and his brothers and sisters saved their money and secretly bought gifts for their new house. That Christmas, their parents shed tears of joy.

"FOR THE FIRST TIME IN MY LIFE, I COULD FEEL THE GRASS GROWING UNDER MY FEET IN A YARD THAT WE OWNED."

Although Ruth was busy raising a family, she found time to become a preacher. On Monday nights, seven or eight women gathered in her basement to sing, pray, and testify. That prayer band grew into a small church, Victory Prayer Chapel.

Although the Cummingses struggled to feed their family, they taught their children to share. Elijah's mother cooked and cleaned for sick neighbors and gave homemade canned goods to hungry families.

Elijah saw his parents' example as faith in action. "One of their callings as children of God was to take care of those in need."

"MY MOTHER WAS ONE OF THE SMARTEST, MOST THOUGHTFUL AND LOVING PEOPLE I HAVE EVER KNOWN. SHE CREATED A HOME FOR ME, MY DAD, AND MY SIX SIBLINGS WHERE GOD WAS AT THE CENTER AND LOVE OVERFLOWED."

Some weekends, the Cummings family, dressed in their Sunday best, headed to Friendship Airport. Not to go on trips, but to watch planes take off and land.

"MY FATHER WAS
A GREAT INSPIRATION
TO ME. HE TAUGHT
US NOTHING
WAS IMPOSSIBLE."

At age nine, Elijah took his first job—as a paperboy for the *Afro-American* newspaper. The editor encouraged Elijah to go to college.

After church on Sundays, Elijah ran home to listen to Rev. Martin Luther King's speeches on his transistor radio. Dr. King's words opened Elijah's heart and eyes. In his neighborhood, he noticed that some boys like him—African American and working class—were not in school. Instead, they were in reform school for running afoul of the law. But they were just kids, not hardened criminals.

As Elijah watched the television lawyer Perry Mason, he recalled the real-life civil rights lawyer Juanita Jackson Mitchell. It dawned on him that those boys needed defending.

"WE HAVE A MORAL RESPONSIBILITY TO DO EVERYTHING IN OUR POWER TO HELP PEOPLE LIVE THE BEST LIVES THAT THEY CAN."

"I SAY TO OUR CHILDREN,
DON'T LET ANYBODY
TAKE AWAY YOUR HOPE.
I DON'T CARE WHO THEY ARE.
AND LET NO ONE
DEFINE YOU. NO ONE."

By high school, Elijah had chosen his profession: law. But his school counselor tried to dash his dream. "Who do you think you are? Your momma is a domestic and your daddy is a laborer," the counselor reminded Elijah. He was shattered.

That evening, he told his mother what happened. "Have faith," she said. "God has a plan for you."

While in school, Elijah worked at a drugstore. The pharmacist, Albert Friedman, gave him the money to apply to college and regularly sent him notes saying "Hang in there," along with ten dollars. That show of faith was not lost on Elijah.

"EDUCATION IS THE GATEWAY FOR SUCCESS IN ACCOMPLISHING ANYTHING IN LIFE."

Elijah was outgoing, but his religion was strict.
And his parents had rules: No card games, period.
When he danced for the first time, it was at his
high school prom.

At Howard University, in Washington, DC, Elijah became a campus leader. He was the president of his sophomore class and, later, of the student government. Elijah graduated with honors and went to law school in 1973.

He was working as a lawyer when he was elected to the Maryland House of Delegates in 1983. Concerned that children could be harmed, he championed a ban on alcohol and tobacco advertising in inner-city neighborhoods.

"FOR GENERATIONS, COUNTLESS AFRICAN AMERICANS HAVE SPOKEN UP WHEN THEY SEE INJUSTICE, AND IT IS IN THEIR MEMORY THAT WE FIGHT TO PROTECT OUR PROGRESS TODAY. NOT JUST FOR OURSELVES, BUT FOR GENERATIONS YET UNBORN."

"OUR NATION'S CIVIL RIGHTS STRUGGLES ARE NOT LIMITED TO OUR HISTORY. NOW, WE ARE THE AMERICANS WHO MUST ORGANIZE, MOBILIZE, AND FIGHT THE GOOD FIGHT."

Elijah was more than a public figure. He was also a father of three. Just as his own parents uplifted him, he praised his children as Black, brilliant, and beautiful.

In 1996, Elijah Cummings was elected to the U.S. House of Representatives. Fellow lawmakers looked up to him, and in 2003, he was elected chair of the Congressional Black Caucus. Elijah was now a voice for people of color. He spoke out to ensure that everyone was treated fairly and equally.

Although he was a Washington power broker, Elijah never left his roots, commuting to the Capitol from his inner-city Baltimore neighborhood. He kept a campaign sign in his home's window so citizens could find him if they needed help.

In 2015, when police brutality sparked protests in Baltimore, Elijah rushed to the scene of the unrest with his bullhorn. He called for calm. Then this son of preachers walked arm in arm with residents, singing an African American spiritual: "This little light of mine, I'm gonna let it shine."

"WE HAVE BEEN CHOSEN TO LIGHT THE WAY FOR OUR NEIGHBORS."

"IN GOD'S TIME,
WE SHALL OVERCOME."

In Congress, Elijah was a beacon for justice, rising to become chair of the House Committee on Oversight and Reform in 2019. With a cool head, a booming voice, and a sense of history, he pushed for change even though he was battling ill health and relied on a cane and a walker.

A relentless warrior, Elijah Cummings was always working for tomorrow—and for youth. "Our children," he said, "are the living messages we send to a future we will never see."

EXCERPT OF STATEMENT FROM THE CONGRESSIONAL BLACK CAUCUS

October 17, 2019

As a lifelong advocate for justice, equality, and the truth, Elijah Cummings was the true definition of a leader, and his commitment to civility and humanity was invaluable. . . .

Born and raised in Baltimore, Maryland, to sharecroppers from South Carolina, Elijah knew firsthand the challenges of discrimination, segregation, and poverty. But at the young age of eleven, he stepped into his calling by helping to integrate a local swimming pool while being attacked with bottles and rocks. This only strengthened his commitment to ensuring his community overcame these obstacles. Once elected to the Maryland House of Delegates, Elijah became the youngest chairman of the Legislative Black Caucus and the first African American to serve as speaker pro tempore.

As the chairman of the House Committee on Oversight and Reform, Elijah used his gavel to speak truth to power on behalf of the American people. Moreover, his fairness and integrity were undeniable by Members on both sides of the aisle. As a former chair of the CBC and an active member within the Caucus, Elijah worked fiercely to uplift and empower Black people. He shared his wisdom and strength in his ongoing efforts to ensure Black Americans received equal rights and protection under the law. Simply put, Elijah was a civil rights icon.

TIMELINE

1951 Elijah Eugene Cummings is born January 18 in Baltimore to former sharecroppers Ruth Elma (née Cochran) and Robert Cummings. **1962** At age eleven, joins protests to desegregate a swimming pool in Baltimore. **1969** Graduates with honors from Baltimore City College High School. **1973** Obtains his bachelor's degree in political science from Howard University, graduating with honors. **1976** Graduates from the University of Maryland School of Law and receives his Juris Doctor degree. Is admitted to the bar on his first try. **1983** Is sworn into the Maryland House of Delegates, where he serves for fourteen years. **1994** Is diagnosed with a rare cancer, thymic carcinoma. **1995** Becomes the state's first African American speaker pro tempore, who presides over the House of Delegates when the speaker is absent. **1996** Wins a seat in the US House of Representatives in a special election and later the general election. He holds his seat until his passing. **2003** Is elected chair of the Congressional Black Caucus. **2008** Marries Maya Rockeymoore. Co-chairs Barack Obama's Maryland state campaign in his first presidential election. **2015** Speaks in Baltimore at the funeral of Freddie Gray, who died after the police used excessive force. **2016** Announces his endorsement of Hillary Clinton for president. **2017** Undergoes heart surgery at Johns Hopkins Hospital. Is awarded his thirteenth and final honorary doctorate, from the University of Maryland, College Park. **2019** Is elected chair of the House Committee on Oversight and Reform. Undergoes an unspecified medical procedure. Issues a statement supporting the impeachment of President Donald Trump. Congressman Elijah Cummings passes away at age sixty-eight, becoming the first African American legislator to lie in state in the US Capitol.

BIBLIOGRAPHY

Barker, Jeff. "Rep. Elijah Cummings Rose from Segregated Childhood to Powerful Political Voice in Baltimore, Washington." *The Baltimore Sun,* Oct. 17, 2019. (baltimoresun.com/politics/bs-md-pol-cummings-dies-20191017-bbwnrp72nndejatug3v7rj2zga-story.html)

Cornish, Stephanie. "Advancing Dr. King's Vision for Peace." *Afro,* Jan. 6, 2016. (afro.com/advancing-dr-kings-vision-for-peace)

Cummings, Elijah. "Elijah Cummings . . . What Kind of America?" *Afro,* Mar. 16, 2011. (afro.com/elijah-cummings-what-kind-of-america)

Cummings, Elijah. "Gifts of the Heart." *Afro,* Dec. 12, 2012. (afro.com/gifts-of-the-heart)

Cummings, Elijah. "A History Lesson for Our Time." *Afro,* Feb. 28, 2019. (afro.com/a-history-lesson-for-our-time)

Cummings, Elijah. Interview on *60 Minutes,* CBS, Jan. 13, 2019. (cbsnews.com/video/elijah-cummings-new-power-as-house-oversight-committee-chairman-60-minutes)

Cummings, Elijah. Keynote speech at American Bar Association Spring Conference, Baltimore, Apr. 12, 2019. (americanbar.org/groups/crsj/events_cle/2019-crsj-spring-meeting/cummings-remarks-2019-spring)

Cummings, Elijah. "We Create the 'History' Our Children Will Remember." *Afro,* Feb. 1, 2012. (afro.com/we-create-the-history-our-children-will-remember)

Howard University Office of Communications. "The Passing of the Honorable Elijah E. Cummings." Oct. 17, 2019. (newsroom.howard.edu/newsroom/static/11371/passing-honorable-elijah-e-cummings)

March Funeral Homes. "The Honorable Elijah Eugene Cummings." Oct. 25, 2019. (marchfh.com/download/129986/Cummings_Elijah1.pdf)

McBride, Jessica. "Elijah Cummings Quotes: Words to Remember the Leader By." *Heavy,* Oct. 17, 2019. (heavy.com/news/2019/10/elijah-cummings-quotes)

Owens, Donna. "Congressman Elijah Cummings: A Baltimore Original." BET, Oct. 19, 2019. (bet.com/news/national/2019/10/19/elijah-cummings-a-baltimore-original.html)

Portnoy, Jenna. "Elijah Cummings, Baltimore Congressman and Civil Rights Leader, Dies at 68." *The Washington Post,* Oct. 17, 2019. (washingtonpost.com/nation/2019/10/17/elijah-cummings-dies-baltimore)

Rasmussen, Frederick N. "Ruth Cummings, Mother of U.S. Rep. Elijah Cummings and Founder of Victory Prayer Chapel, Dies." *The Baltimore Sun,* Feb. 7, 2018. (baltimoresun.com/obituaries/bs-md-ob-20180207-story.html)

Terris, B. "Elijah Cummings Endured Two Painful Years. Soon He'll Be More Powerful than Ever." *The Washington Post,* Nov. 19, 2018. (washingtonpost.com/lifestyle/style/elijah-cummings-endured-two-painful-years-soon-hell-be-more-powerful-than-ever/2018/11/16/a83805)

Thomas-Lester, Avis. "Paperboys and Papergirls Feted." *Afro,* July 25, 2012. (afro.com/paperboys-and-papergirls-feted)

Tynes, Tyler. "The Giant Life of Elijah Cummings." *The Ringer,* Oct. 17, 2019. (theringer.com/2019/10/17/20919761/representative-elijah-cummings-obituary)

QUOTE SOURCES

This is our (back cover): Elijah Cummings column, *The Afro,* 8/12/2015 • **I had rights:** Elijah Cummings's Facebook page, 8/14/2016 • **They had faith:** Elijah Cummings Congressional Office press release, 7/26/2015–7/29/2015 (Union of Black Episcopalians speech) • **My mom and:** *Baltimore Sun,* 2/7/2018, bsun.md/2EPgqoX • **The librarians and:** Elijah Cummings column, *The Afro,* 2/1/2012 • **For the first:** Elijah Cummings column, *The Afro,* 2/12/2012 • **My mother was:** *Baltimore Sun,* 2/7/2018, bsun.md/2EPgqoX • **My father was:** *Baltimore Sun,* 6/10/2000, baltimoresun.com/news/bs-xpm-2000-06-10-0006100090-story.html • **We have a:** Elijah Cummings Congressional Office press release, 9/24/2015 • **I say to:** *USA Today,* 8/3/2019 • **Education is the:** Cedric Richmond Congressional Office press release, 5/7/2019 • **For generations, countless:** Elijah Cummings Congressional Office press release, 2/1/2017 • **Our nation's civil:** Elijah Cummings column, *The Afro,* 2/12/2014 • **We have been:** Elijah Cummings Congressional Office press release, 7/26/2015–7/29/2015 (Union of Black Episcopalians speech) • **In God's time:** Elijah Cummings Congressional Office press release, 7/26/2015–7/29/2015 (Union of Black Episcopalians speech)